Finding Out About
VICTORIAN SOCIAL
REFORMERS

Michael Rawcliffe

B.T. Batsford Limited, London

Contents

Frontispiece

Poor children on arrival at Dr Barnado's (Barnardo Photographic Archive).

Cover illustrations

The colour illustration is a section of the frontispiece from In Darkest England and the Way Out *by William Booth; the black and white photograph shows a nineteenth-century Newcastle street scene; the advertisement for Dr Barnardo's Homes is from* Whitaker's Almanac (*1886*).

© Michael Rawcliffe 1987
First published 1987

Typeset by Tek-Art Ltd, Kent
and printed in Great Britain by
R J Acford Ltd,
Chichester, Sussex
for the publishers
B.T. Batsford Limited,
4 Fitzhardinge Street
London W1H 0AH

ISBN 0 7134 5051 7

ACKNOWLEDGMENTS

The Author and Publishers would like to thank the following for kind permission to reproduce illustrations: Barnardo Photographic Archive for the frontispiece; Heatherbank Museum of Social Work, Glasgow, for page 8 (bottom); The Post Office for pages 3 and 24; Punch Publications for page 40; The National Trust Photographic Library for page 22; The Salvation Army for pages 5, 10, 12, 13 and 42 (left); Wellcome Institute Library, London, for page 33. The remaining illustrations are from the Author's collection.

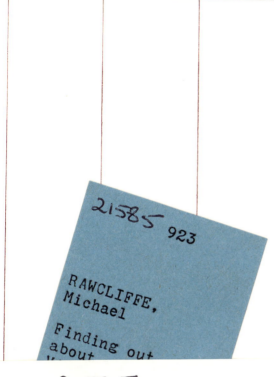

Introduction

This book is about men and women who helped to bring about important changes during the reign of Queen Victoria (1837-1901). The choice made is a personal one, and whilst some of those included would appear in most historians' lists, some of them would not. This is not particularly strange, for if I asked ten people to list the most important people in this century, or the ten best books, or films, there would be many variations.

My aim has been to choose a broad variety of individuals who helped bring about changes in the lives of other men and women during the Victorian period. Some of these are included because they brought a particular injustice or problem to the surface. Thus, I have included the authors Charles Dickens and Charles Kingsley, whose fictional works were often based on their investigations amongst the poor.

Others were employed as journalists or reporters, giving factual accounts and through their writings outlining the particular problem in the daily press or in magazines. Henry Mayhew, a journalist, James Greenwood, a writer, and Seebohm Rowntree and Charles Booth as social investigators, all exposed the conditions under which the poor lived. The detail which they provided not only alerted the better off to the problems of housing, unemployment, low pay, insufficient food and disease suffered by the poor, but also brought the problems to the attention of Parliament.

Two of the women included, Annie Besant and Beatrice Webb, were concerned with the working conditions of women in the sweated industries, where the Factory Acts did not apply. Both were able to influence not only the general public but also Parliament, and Beatrice Webb gave evidence to several Select Committees established by Parliament.

Today it is assumed that the State will help those in society who are unable to help themselves, and that laws will be passed by Parliament, and bye-laws by local councils, which will ensure that minimum standards of such things as health, safety and buildings are observed. This was not always the case in the nineteenth century. Many people believed that Government should not interfere at all in the lives of the people, and that Government's main purpose was to defend the country and enable people to help themselves, or *allow* towns and cities to introduce various improvement schemes. Not only were the majority unwilling to see their taxes used to help the poor and sick, but at the local level increased rates for improvements frequently met with opposition.

Only four of the 18 reformers included are women. This is not because I happen to be a male, but rather that opportunities for women were limited in the nineteenth century. Women did not have the vote, and only later in the century were they able to enter many of the professions.

Each double page gives no more than a glimpse of the work in which each individual was involved. I hope that the book will inspire you to find out more about them and also to suggest others who might have been included.

Stamps issued by the Post Office. Design a stamp for another reformer mentioned in the book.

Much will depend on where you live and whether or not you have access to a good library. Most towns have a reference library and the larger ones a local history section, or even a record office, where all the local records are kept. Do check the opening hours before you travel any distance and ask at school to find whether or not you need a letter of introduction. Take a notebook and pencil with you. Ink pens and biros are often forbidden as they might harm the documents. The following list should help you to be aware of the type of material that will be available.

1. WRITTEN MATERIAL

a) *Autobiographies* Famous people often wrote their memoirs or autobiographies in later life. Some are based on their diaries. For example, Beatrice Webb wrote *My Apprenticeship* (1926), which was largely based on her diaries. Look up when she was born and suggest why we must always be on our guard when we are reading about events written up much later, by one who was involved.

b) *Biographies* Many famous people have been the subject of biographies. Sometimes the family loan important documents to the biographer after the individual has died. The better biographers will indicate where their material came from. Remember that biographies will vary in their approach and the same person may be praised by one writer and criticized by another. Why is this?

c) *Newspapers* Newspapers are an excellent source and *The Times* index will give you the day on which an obituary appeared in the paper. This will be a good starting point for your investigation, for it will highlight the major events with which the individual was concerned. You will then be able to check these in the national press. Most libraries have back copies of *The Times* and their own local newspapers. For example, the local Bradford papers are very useful for finding out more about Titus Salt.

d) *Magazines* These were very popular in Victorian times. The humorous weekly magazine *Punch* was first published in 1840 and contains many excellent cartoons. The other magazine which is still fairly common is the *Illustrated London News*, which was published weekly (now monthly). It was particularly popular because of its excellent line drawings, before newspapers contained photographs.

e) *Fiction* Many Victorian novels were first published in part-form or as serials in magazines. The popular ones were often read aloud and "penny readings" were a common form of entertainment. Sometimes an author would be there to read parts of his or her novel (Dickens was in great demand). "Penny readings" also provided warmth and company for those from the poorer areas.

One must use fiction carefully. There are several books by authors such as Mrs Gaskell, Charles Kingsley, Charles Dickens and Thomas Hardy which contain descriptions based upon their observations. Remember, though, that a novel is a work of imagination and that the author may also be seeking to win over the reader to a particular cause.

f) *Census material* The census dates from 1801, and you will find the detailed census from 1841 particularly useful if you are enquiring into housing densities and the occupations of those living in the slums. The census is subject to a "100-year rule" which forbids detail being made public until a 100 years have elapsed. Why do you think this is?

g) *Guides and directories* Local guidebooks and county or town directories are very useful if you want to find details of an area at a particular time.

h) *Other reference books* The Dictionary of National Biography is available in most reference libraries and gives detailed biographies of famous people. Each article is followed by a book list.

i) *Government reports* The Victorians established many Government enquiries in either the House of Commons or the House of Lords. These Select Committees investigated particular problems, e.g. housing conditions of the working class, or conditions of women and children in coal mines. Their findings were published and contain interviews conducted with witnesses, letters, reports from specialists and sometimes maps, sketches or diagrams.

2. VISUAL MATERIAL

a) *Photographs and prints* Many libraries have a print and photograph collection, and you will find illustrations from various libraries reproduced in many books. They are very useful in giving you the feel of what it must have been like to have worked in the mines as a young child or to have grown up in the slums in damp and overcrowded conditions. Remember that photographs were often posed and that they were taken for a purpose. Dr Barnardo often used photographs of poor children as a means of appealing for money (see the frontispiece to this book).

b) *Maps* Large-scale Ordnance Survey maps of the Victorian period (at 6 in. and 25 in. to the mile) will help you to recreate areas which have now been redeveloped. You will also be able to identify particular streets or courts which are listed in the census.

c) *Objects* Medals and pottery were often produced to commemorate the death or anniversary of a particular social reformer. Local museums may have a small collection, and they are an indication of the gratitude that many felt for the changes that they helped bring about. On our £10 note you will find one of the social reformers mentioned in this book.

d) *Street and town names* Though less popular than kings and queens, reformers such as Dickens and Shaftesbury have often been used, particularly in their home area. Dickens is particularly associated with Kent and London, whilst Shaftesbury has Shaftesbury Avenue in London named after him.

An advertisement for William Booth's book in the newspaper The War Cry, *October 1890.*

Dr Barnardo and Children's Homes

The population of our towns and cities increased rapidly in the nineteenth century and cheap rented accommodation was in short supply. Many were forced to live on the streets, and their numbers were swelled by abandoned children.

THE EVENT THAT CHANGED HIS LIFE

In *The Christian* of 1868 Dr Barnardo described how, as a young student he had met Jim Jarvis two years previously at an evening school for poor children in Stepney.

> "Come, my lad, it's time to go home now.
> Please sir, let me stop.
> Stop! What for? You ought to go home at once. Your mother will wonder what keeps you out so late.
> I ain't got no mother.
> But your father, where's he?
> I ain't got no father.
> Stuff and nonsense, boy. Don't tell me such stories! Where do you live? And where are your friends?
> Ain't got no friends. Don't live nowhere.
> . . . Where did you sleep last night?
> Down in Whitechapel, along of the 'Ay Market, in one of them carts filled with 'ay.
> . . . Are there other boys like you in London, without homes or friends?
> Oh yes, sir, lots – 'eaps on em."
>
> I gave him hot coffee and was taken to the Market.

Why do you think Dr Barnardo was so surprised that the boy had no home?

Jim Jarvis showing Dr Barnardo a group of homeless boys asleep on a house roof in November 1866. The picture comes from Memoirs of the Late Dr Barnardo. *How accurate do you think this is as a source?* ▶

THE FIRST HOME

Soon his studies began to suffer. In 1868 he rented a room in Bale Street, Stepney, and spent the evenings finding homeless children and putting them into lodgings. It was not long before he decided to make this his life's work. In his memoir entry for 1870 he described his first home for the homeless at 18 Stepney Causeway in the East End of London.

> **Many a happy hour was spent in whitewashing walls and ceilings, scrubbing floors, and otherwise putting the place into a suitable condition for the reception of my first family. Then I spent two whole nights upon the streets of London, cast my net . . . and brought to shore 25 homeless lads all willing and eager to accept such help as I could give them.**

Why did Barnardo go out at night to search for suitable children?

THE EDINBURGH CASTLE

The Edinburgh Castle was a gin palace and music hall in the East End of London. Nearby, Barnardo erected a tent which could hold 3000 people. From there he preached the evils of drink and urged people to sign the Pledge (of abstinence). In a letter to *The Christian* in 1872 he described how

> . . . a public house a short distance away was closed, almost in the middle of our work; then another followed. The Edinburgh Castle was in the centre of the very district we were affecting. At length the licensee found he could not carry on his business, and the brewers were determined to put him out. He was so indignant at what he thought was the shabby way he had been treated, that he came to me and said, will you buy my house and business?

Within a month Barnardo had raised the purchase money of £4000 and soon converted it into a "Coffee Palace".

Why did many Christians such as Barnardo think that drink was an evil, especially for the poor?

The Edinburgh Castle after it had been opened as a mission church and coffee palace in 1872. ▼

A HOME FOR GIRLS

In 1873 Barnardo married and was given a house at Barkingside in Essex as a wedding present. This he extended and in 1875 he took in 60 homeless girls. However he soon began to have doubts, which he outlined at the first Annual General Meeting on the 31 March 1875:

> Among my first thirty girls I had as many depraved [corrupt] children gathered in our little home as I suppose have ever been aggregated [gathered together] under one roof since then. These were mostly criminals in embryo [in the making], the offspring of degraded and vicious women.

This led him to introduce the family system, which he later described in his own unpublished memoir.

> There should be no longer a great house in which sixty of these motherless girls would be herded together, clad in some dull uniform generally divested of all prettiness; but little cottages should arise, each of them presided over by its own "mother", and in which all members of the family could be clad as working people's children were under ordinary circumstances . . . . There family life and family love might be reproduced, and gentle, modest ways would be made possible . . . under the influence of godly women whom I was sure would come to my aid in good time.

Why did he feel that the cottage system was preferable to all the girls living under one roof? In which would you have chosen to be brought up?

The Dr Barnardo's charity still exists. See if you can find out how the homes are organized today.

Annie Besant and the Matchgirls

Working conditions and low pay were still widespread, especially in the small workshops and industries not covered by the Factory Acts. Many of the poorest paid were women.

An advertisement from Routledge's Guide to London of 1871. Why were the matches advertised as safe?

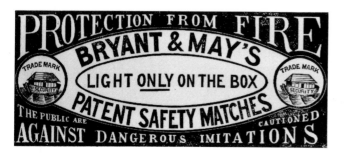

Annie Besant with the strike committee of the union which she helped to found. Which do you think is Annie?

At a meeting of Fabian socialists (see page 44) in June 1888 Annie Besant heard a talk on the poor working conditions of the girls in the Bryant and May match factory at Bromley-by-Bow in the East End of London. Annie visited the factory and decided to write an article for the Socialist paper *The Link*, which she edited. The first article appeared on 7 July 1888:

> The hour for commencing work is 6.30 in summer and 8 in winter; work concludes at 6 p.m. Half an hour is allowed for breakfast and an hour for dinner. This long day is performed by young girls, who have to stand the whole time. A typical case is that of a girl of 16, a piece worker; she earns 4s. a week .... The splendid salary of 4s. is subject to deductions in the shape of fines; if the feet are dirty, or the ground under the bench is left untidy, a fine of 3d. is inflicted; for putting "burnts" – matches that have caught fire during the work – on the bench 1s. has been forfeited .... If a girl leaves four or five matches on her bench when she goes for a fresh "frame" she is fined 3d., and in some departments a fine of 3d. is inflicted for talking. If a girl is late she is shut out for "half a day", that is, for the morning six hours, and 5d. is deducted out of her day's 8d.

Which rules would you have found it most difficult to keep? If a girl earned 8d. a day and 4s. a week, can you work out how many days a week she was working? (If you are not sure how many pennies make a shilling look it up on page 47.)

THE STRIKE

On 14 July 1888 *The Link* published a letter received during the previous week from the matchgirls.

> My Dear Lady – we thank you very much for the kind interest you have taken in us poor girls, and hope that you will succeed in your undertaking. Dear Lady, you need not trouble yourself about the letter I read in the *Link* that Mr. Bryant sent you, because you have spoken the truth, and we are very pleased to read it. Dear Lady, they are trying to get the poor girls to say it is all lies that has been printed, and trying to make them sign papers to say it is lies . . . we will not sign them . . . . We hope you will not get into any trouble in our behalf, as what you have spoke is quite true . . . . Dear Lady, do not mention the date this letter was written and . . . do keep that [our names] as a secret.

In the event a girl was dismissed and 1400 fellow workers went on strike.

What had been Annie Besant's part in the events leading to the strike?

SUCCESS

The matchgirls were supported by the 25,000 members of the London Trades' Council, which sent a deputation to meet the directors of Bryant and May. *The Link* on 21 July 1888 reported the result:

> It was finally agreed that: (1) all fines should be abolished, (2) all deductions for paint, brushes, stamps, etc., should be put an end to, (3) the 3d. should be restored to all packers, (4) the 'pennies' should be restored, . . . (5) all grievances should be laid directly before the firm, ere [before] any hostile action be taken, (6) all girls to be taken back. The firm hoped the girls would form a Union; they promised to see about providing a room for meals away from the work, and they also promised to provide barrows for carrying the boxes, which have been hitherto carried by young girls on their heads, to the great detriment of their hair and their spine.

List the points in the order of importance from the point of view of the matchgirls. Which concession do you think Bryant and May would have been most reluctant to concede.?

OPPOSITION FROM THE TIMES

The *Star* believed that the girls had been influenced by "the twaddle of Mrs Besant". *The Times* supported this:

> The pity is that the matchgirls have not been suffered to take their own course, but have been egged on to strike by irresponsible advisers. No effort has been spared by these pests of the modern industrial world, the Social Democrats, to bring the quarrel to a head.

The Times believed that the strike was bound to fail and that the girls would either return to work or go to jobs elsewhere.

What does *The Times* accuse Annie Besant of doing?

Charles Booth and the Survey of London

Charles Booth was concerned about poverty and unemployment in London in the 1880s. However, he believed that the figure of 25 per cent poverty quoted in a recent survey was exaggerated and he set out to challenge it. In fact, he found that it was an underestimate and that roughly one in three was living in poverty.

THE INVESTIGATION BEGINS

In 1886 Booth set up the Board of Statistical Research. One of its members was Beatrice Webb, about whom you can read on pages 40-1. Beatrice Webb in her diary recalls the first meeting:

> **17 April, 1886** (York House)
> **Object of the Committee [is] to get a fair picture of the whole of London society – the 4,000,000 – by district and employment, the two methods to be based on census returns. We passed Charles Booth's elaborate and detailed plan for the work, and a short abstract of it for general purposes.**
>
> **At present Charles Booth is the sole worker in this gigantic undertaking. If I were more advanced in knowledge of previous conditions, just the sort of work I should like to undertake – and if I were free! But I intend to do a little bit of it while I am in London, not only to keep the Society alive, but to keep me in touch with *actual facts* so as to limit my study of the past to that part of it useful in the understanding of the present.**

Which was the most recent census available to Charles Booth which would have given the general figures? His first two studies on the *Life and Labour of the People in London* were published in 1889 and 1891 and these two volumes were followed by another 15.

THE EIGHT CLASSES

Booth divided the population of the East End into eight classes:

A **The lowest class of occasional labourers, loafers and semi-criminals**
B **Casual earnings – "very poor"**
C **Intermittent**   ⎫ together
D **Small regular earnings** ⎬ "the Poor"
E **Regular standard earnings – above the line of poverty**
F **Higher class labour**
G **Lower Middle Class**
H **Upper Middle Class**

Why did Booth believe that A – D were in poverty? Initially he and his team of investigators worked in the East End, but then he wondered whether other parts of London were as poor. Sadly, he found that the West End of London had as many poor as the East.

A mother making brush heads at home. How can ▲ you tell that this family is poor? How might Booth have classified them?

A section from Charles Booth's Poverty Maps of 1889. The original maps were coloured according to the levels of poverty Booth found in different areas. ▶

MRS PIERCE

Booth outlined his method of enquiry to Beatrice Webb. In *My Apprenticeship* (1926) she quotes him as saying,

> The root idea with which I began the work was that every fact I needed was known to someone, and that the information had simply to be collected and put together.

An example of his careful and detailed recording is to be found in Booth's own notebook quoted by his daughter, Mary Booth, in *Charles Booth, a Memoir* (1918):

> Mrs Pierce's husband has been dead a good many years, and, besides son and brother-in-law, she has living upstairs in this house a married daughter and her husband, whose little girl it is that sits on Mr Pierce's knee, making dangerous play with his knife when she can get it. She is three years old, but small and backward – can't talk at all beyond saying "ta", and can barely walk, it seems, having had very bad health – one sickness after another for months together.

Why would such detailed recording be useful?

SHELTON STREET

Booth and his interviewers considered families in relation to their street and neighbourhood. In this extract from *Life and Labour of the People in London* (1891) he describes Shelton Street.

> . . . Shelton Street was just wide enough for a vehicle to pass either way, with room between curb-stone and houses for one foot-passenger to walk; but vehicles would pass seldom, and foot-passengers would prefer the roadway to the risk of tearing their clothes against projecting nails. The houses, about forty in number, contained cellars, parlours, and first, second, and third floors, mostly two rooms on a floor, and few of the 200 families who lived here occupied more than one room. In little rooms no more than 8ft square, would be found living father, mother, and several children . . . . Most of the people described are Irish Roman Catholics getting a living as market porters, or by selling flowers, fruit, fowls, or vegetables in the streets, but as to not a few it is a mystery how they live. Drunkenness and dirt and bad language prevailed, and violence was common, reaching at times even to murder.

Can you guess into which class Booth placed the street?

11

William Booth and the Salvation Army

William Booth began mission work in London in 1865 and became an evangelist, taking Christianity to the people in the streets and public houses of the poor areas. In 1878 he founded the Salvation Army. Evangelists became captains and lieutenants and members became "soldiers".

MY VISIT TO CARDIFF

In the first issue of the Salvation Army's magazine, *The Deliverer*, on 1 July 1889, Mrs Booth described her visit to the South Wales port:

> I was much impressed during my visit to Cardiff with the terrible need of Rescue work in that city – seaports are all, or nearly all, cesspools of drunkenness and immorality. This seems to me more than usual a field of temptation at Cardiff. I hope the Royal Commission which was at work during my visit will find out a remedy, but I doubt it.
>
> Our Rescue work there though still small is good – funds are very low and the officers much burdened on that account, the house is not the most convenient, and the class of girls rescued is very rough but there has been blessed success, and I believe the Lord's people in the town are awakened to new interests in the work.

You can see how the Salvation Army was concerned not only with bringing people to Christianity but also with helping people. What problems were faced by the officers in Cardiff?

The Salvation Army had their own match factory. ▶ *What advantages do they offer their workers? After what date must this advertisement have been produced?*

DECOYED OR STRAYED

Mrs Booth also organized an Enquiry and Help Department. *The Deliverer* on 15 August 1889 contained the following advertisement.

DECOYED OR STRAYED

On Good Friday last a little girl of 10 or 11 years, named PHILLCOCKS, disappeared from 39, Colley Street, West Bromwich. Her parents are heartbroken by her prolonged absence, and fear the worst that could happen to her.

Appearance: dark blue eyes, with a slight cross, brown hair, rather thin face, mark on thigh, height 3 feet 9 inches. Information to be addressed to Enquiry, 259 Mare Street, Hackney, NE.

How many months had the child been absent? How would the parents try and find their lost child today?

Poor children queueing outside a Salvation Army ▶ *hostel for breakfast in 1880. Can you see the Salvation Army Officer?*

THE SUBMERGED TENTH

In 1890 William Booth published *In Darkest England and the Way Out*. He had been very much influenced by Charles Booth's survey and also his own observations.

> **The foul and fetid breath of our slums is almost as poisonous as that of Africa. Fever is almost as chronic there as at the Equator . . . . A population sodden with drink, steeped in Vice; eaten up by every sort of social and physical malady, these are the denizens [inhabitants] of Darkest England amidst whom my life has been spent . . .**
>
> **Darkest England . . . may be said to have a population equal to that of Scotland. Three million men, women and children, a vast despairing multitude in a condition nominally free, but really enslaved; . . . these it is whom we have to save . . . The Submerged Tenth . . .**

The explorer H.M. Stanley had recently written a book entitled *In Darkest Africa* and so Booth's title would have had an immediate appeal. But since Booth had never been to Africa himself do you think his comparison a valid one? What impact do you think this piece of writing would have had upon its readers?

AN OUTDOOR MEETING

This description of a Salvation Army meeting comes from George Sims's *Living in London*, published in 1906:

> **Half of them [members of the Salvation Army] are there to speak or sing only, the other half blow or beat lustily at musical instruments, even two of the women, in their neat blue uniform dresses and scoop bonnets, playing cornets . . . the last hymn is scarcely ended when one of the wearers of red jerseys – a wan, eager young man – bares his head, and stepping to the centre of the ring shouts an impassioned prayer with his face turned heavenward; then, beseeching the bystanders to go with them to their "citadel" [Chapel] he makes a sign at which his comrades promptly fall into marching order, and with the flag fluttering, drums thumping, and brasses braying, away they sweep, keeping step, up the road.**

Why do you think that the Salvation Army went out into the streets to hold open-air meetings? Why would the brass band have been so effective? How can you tell from these extracts that the writer approves of the Salvation Army?

Edwin Chadwick and Public Health

Few people did more than Edwin Chadwick to publicize the conditions under which many of the poor lived. He had been largely responsible for the Poor Law Amendment Act of 1834 and it was the Poor Law unions which provided the information for the *Report on the Conditions of the Labouring Population in England and Wales* (1842), which was written mainly by Chadwick.

THE 1842 REPORT

This report was one of the most widely read books in Victorian England: its impact was even greater because it contained not only detailed descriptions backed up by figures, but also plans and illustrations. Two of the Reports major conclusions were,

First, as to the extent and operation of the evils which are the subject of the inquiry

That the formation of all habits of cleanliness is obstructed by defective supplies of water. That the annual loss of life from filth and bad ventilation are greater than the loss from death or wounds in all the wars in which the country has been engaged in modern times.

Secondly, as to the means by which the present sanitary conditions of the labouring classes may be improved

The primary and most important measures, and at the same time the most practicable, and within the recognised province of public administration, are drainage, the removal of habitations [houses], streets, and roads, and the improvement of the supplies of water.

That for all these purposes, as well as

OPPOSITION TO CHANGE

S.E. Finer, in *The Life and Times of Sir Edwin Chadwick* (1952), refers to an undated letter of Chadwick's, written in 1852, in which he attacks the opponents of change,

... who from ignorance resist measures by which even their own property would be improved .... These men are amongst the foremost agitators for reform in every administration but their own: they are the protectionists and defenders of filth.

Next to these are the shareholders and connexion of shareholders in bad water companies, who profit by the monopoly of inferior supplies; chimney owners who talk of political enlightenment and befoul the population with soot; shareholders and connexions and foul trading interests, as well as the class of owners of ill-conditioned tenements for which exorbitant [unreasonably high] rents are exacted.

List the various groups named by Chadwick and try and work out why each, for different reasons, was opposed to improvements in public health.

An artist's impression of the slums of St Giles, ▶ London (c. 1852). How many dangers to health can you see in this picture?

domestic use, better supplies of water are absolutely necessary.

What does Chadwick regard as the biggest obstacle to improvement and what are the three most important means by which improvement could be made?

By 1854 Chadwick had made many enemies and was forced to retire, on a small pension, from public life. *The Times* was not sorry to see him go, as is shown in this extract from 8 July 1854:

> **Future historians who want to know what a Commission, a Board, whether national or local, a secretary, whether working or parliamentary, a Report, a secretary of state or almost any member of our system was in the nineteenth century, will find the name of Chadwick inextricably mixed up with the inquiries .... Ask, Who did this? Who wrote that? Who made this index or that dietary? Who manages that appointment, or order that sewer, and the answer is the same – Mr. Edwin Chadwick.**

The Times shows a grudging admiration for the man but implies that he interfered in everyone's business. Compare this extract with the one that follows, which highlights his achievements:

> **Mr. Chadwick has no doubt done more than any other man in direct furtherance of the general health. He has looked at the subject on every side, and exhibited it in every light. He has insisted, not only on the cruelty of condemning a multitude of our citizens to disease and premature death . . . but on the sin of encouraging crime by discomfort . . . he has so strenuously worked the enterprise of reform, that its completion is, amidst many discouragements and difficulties, natural in such a case, merely a question of time.** (Harriet Martineau, *The History of the Peace, 1815-46,* 1858)

Eventually, Chadwick's achievements were recognized when in 1889, a year before his death, he was knighted.

In spite of Chadwick's work this illustration from a book of 1881 is still warning people about a major health hazard. What is it?

Joseph Chamberlain: a Reforming Mayor

Joseph Chamberlain was Mayor of Birmingham in the 1870s and was determined to govern the city in the best interests of the people.

A postcard of Mr and Mrs Chamberlain. The original photograph was taken in 1888, but the postcard is Edwardian and was posted in 1906. So be warned! ▶

WHAT LOCAL GOVERNMENT CAN DO

R.W. Dale, in his book *The Laws of Christ for Common Life* (1884), expressed Joseph Chamberlain's view that local politicians can often do much to settle the major issues concerning the individual:

> I sometimes think that municipalities can do more for the people than Parliament. Their powers will probably be enlarged; but under the powers they already possess they can greatly diminish the amount of sickness in the community, and can prolong human life. They can prevent – they have prevented – tens of thousands of children from becoming orphans. They can do much to improve those miserable homes which are fatal not only to health, but to decency and morality. They can give to the poor the enjoyment of pleasant parks and gardens, and the intellectual cultivation and refinement of public libraries and galleries of art. They can redress [put right] in many ways the inequalities of human conditions.

What does the author think can be achieved by local government? Were the parks, galleries and libraries in your town founded in Victorian times?

TAKING OVER THE GAS COMPANIES

Birmingham's problems were vast, but basically concerned poor housing, inadequate water supply and unsatisfactory sewage disposal. Chamberlain joined the council in 1870 and three years later became Mayor. He immediately set about improving the health of the city. Asa Briggs, in *Victorian Cities* (1963), outlines Chamberlain's plan:

> When the purchase of the water works comes before you, it will be a question concerning the health of the town; the acquisition of the Gas Works concerns the profits of the town, – and its financial resources. Both are matters of absolute public necessity.

Chamberlain fought the gas companies and took them over. In the first year the city made £34,000 profit. This enabled the gas supply to be extended and prices lowered. What would have been the disadvantages of several private companies supplying gas to the consumer and why do you think the companies did not want to be taken over?

IMPROVED WATER SUPPLY

In 1874 Joseph Chamberlain began his attack on the privately owned water companies. The death rate for Birmingham was above the national average and a smallpox outbreak in 1874 created an atmosphere supportive of reform. Chamberlain asked:

> **What do you think of the inhabitants being compelled to drink water which is as bad as sewage before clarification?**

In fact, the Royal Commission in Sanitary Reform had reported in 1869 that

> **. . . the power of life and death should above all not be left in private hands. Whereas there should be a profit made on the gas undertaking, the waterworks should never be a source of profit, as all profit should go in the reduction of the price of water.**

Why did the Royal Commission believe that water was more important than gas, and why was a reduction in its price so important?

Birmingham Council gave their support to Chamberlain and in January 1876 the water works were transferred to the Corporation.

WHY I AM A RADICAL REFORMER

In a speech in Birmingham on 12 October 1874 Chamberlain explained his ambitions for reform:

> **I am a Radical Reformer because I would reform and remove ignorance, poverty, intemperance, and crime at their very roots. What is the cause of all this ignorance and vice? Many people say their intemperance is at the bottom of everything and I am not inclined to disagree with them. I believe we hardly ever find misery or poverty without finding that intemperance is one of the factors in such conditions. But at the same time I believe intemperance itself is only an effect produced by causes that lies deeper still. I should say these causes, in the first place, are the gross ignorance of the masses; and in the second place, the horrible shameful homes in which many of the poor are forced to live.**

Why did he argue that intemperance (drink) was as much an effect of the poor conditions under which people lived as the cause?

◀ *Another early twentieth-century postcard, showing Chamberlain Square in Birmingham and several of the recently built improvements.*

Charles Dickens: a Victorian Writer

Charles Dickens was the most popular and widely read author in the nineteenth century. His novels were based upon a close observation of the people and the situations in which they lived. His novels were often first produced as part-magazines on a weekly basis.

THE WORKHOUSE

The cost of poor relief soared in the early nineteenth century and this led to the Poor Law Amendment Act of 1834. Now the stress was on efficiency and economy and the workhouse was to be the place of last resort. You probably know the scene from *Oliver Twist* (1838) in which Oliver asks for more food. Here, in the same novel, Dickens describes the Board of Guardians, the locally elected group responsible for the efficient operation of the Poor Law in their union.

> The members of the board were very sage [wise], deep philosophical men, and when they came to turn their attention to the workhouse, they found out at once, what ordinary folks would never have discovered – the poor people like it! It was a regular place of public entertainment for the poorer classes; a tavern where there was nothing to pay; a public breakfast, dinner, tea, and supper all the year round; a brick and mortar elysium [heaven], where it was all play, and no work . . . they established the rule, that all poor people should have the alternative (for they would compel nobody, not they), of being starved by a gradual process in the house, or by a quick one out of it. With this view they contracted with the waterworks to lay on an unlimited supply of water; and with a corn factor [merchant] to supply periodically small quantities of oatmeal; and issued three meals of this gruel a day, with an onion twice a week, and half a roll on Sundays.

By what means does the author seek to attack those who were interested in nothing more than keeping down the cost of relief?

A CROSSING-SWEEPER

In *Bleak House* (published in weekly parts 1852-3) Dickens introduced a crossing-sweeper called Joe. The boy was based upon George Ruby, who appeared in an assault case at the Guildhall, London on 8 January 1850. He was 14 years old.

Alderman Humphery: Well, do you know what you are about? Do you know what an oath is?

Boy: No.

Alderman: Can you read?

Boy: No.

Alderman: Do you ever say your prayers?

Boy: No.

Alderman: Do you know what prayers are?

Boy: No.

Alderman: Do you know what God is?

Boy: No.

Alderman: Do you know what the devil is?

Boy: No.

Alderman: What do you know?

Boy: I knows how to sweep the crossings.

Alderman: And that's all?

Boy: That's all. I sweeps a crossing.

If Dickens was not at the trial, where else might he have read the account?

A CONTEMPORARY ACCOUNT

Harriet Martineau wrote in *The History of the Peace* (1858):

> Last and greatest among the novelists comes Charles Dickens . . . who rose up in the midst of us like a jin [genie] with his magic glass among some eastern people, showing forth what was doing in the regions of darkness, and in odd places where nobody ever thought of looking. It is scarcely conceivable that any one should, in our age of the world, exert a stronger social influence than Mr. Dickens has in his power. His sympathies are on the side of the suffering and the frail; and this makes him the idol of those who suffer, from whatever cause.

What does the author believe were Dickens' qualities and why does she think he was so powerful?

DICKENS' OBITUARY

This is part of a very long obituary (death notice) which appeared in the *Daily Telegraph* in 1870:

> . . . he knew all about the back streets behind Holborn, the courts and alleys of the Borough, the shabby sidling streets of the remoter suburbs, the crooked little alleys, the city, the dank and oozy wharfs and the water-side. He was at home in all lodging houses, station-houses, cottages, hovels, Cheap-Jack's caravans, workhouses, prisons, school-rooms, chandlers' shops, back attics, barbers' shops, areas, back yards, dark entries, public-houses, rag-shops, police-courts, and markets in poor neighbourhoods.

List some of the evils which were exposed by writing about such topics.

Bluegate Fields, a London slum, as illustrated by Gustave Doré in 1872. This is the sort of area which Dickens often described to his readers.

Dotheboys Hall in Nicholas Nickleby. *What impression is the illustrator "Phiz" seeking to convey to the reader?*

=James Greenwood and the Evils of London

James Greenwood was a journalist and author who set out both to amuse and to inform. He believed that "only by perseveringly and persistently proclaiming the existence of evils . . . one may hope to rouse those who hold the power to apply the proper remedies".

DO NOT BREAK UP A HOME

The Poor Law Amendment Act of 1834 required that a man must sell up his possessions before entering a workhouse, which must be seen as a place of last resort for the poor. In *The Seven Curses of London*, published in the 1870s, Greenwood argues:

> It would be a grand step in the right direction, if a means could be safely adopted that would save a man driven to pauperism from breaking-up his home. The experiment has, it appears, been successfully adopted in Manchester, and may prove generally practicable. The guardians in that city have provided rooms in which the furniture or other household goods of persons compelled to seek a temporary refuge in the house may be stored. It would not do, of course, to enable people to treat the workhouse as a kind of hotel, to which they might retire without inconvenience, and where they might live upon the ratepayers until a pressure has passed. Perhaps the confinement and separation of family-ties which the workhouse involves would sufficiently prevent the privilege being abused . . .

Why does Greenwood believe that the Manchester scheme is a good one? What possible danger does he see in the scheme?

HOW CHILDREN SURVIVE

Many who lived on the streets gathered round the markets for food. In *The Seven Curses of London* (*c.* 1870) Greenwood described Covent Garden in August or September after the wholesale market had finished most of its trade at about eight o'clock.

> They will gather about a muck heap and gobble up plums, a sweltering mass of decay, and oranges and apples that have quite lost their original shape and colour . . . . I have seen one of these gaunt wolfish little children with his tattered cap full of plums of a sort one of which I would not have permitted a child of mine to eat for all the money in the Mint, and this at a season when the sanitary authorities in their desperate alarm at the speed of cholera had turned bill stickers [posters], and were begging and imploring the people to abstain from this, that, and the other, and especially to beware of fruit unless perfectly sound and ripe.

What are the dangers to health for these children?

In *The Wilds of London* (1874) Greenwood deplored the conditions under which the poor lived:

> The sanitory conditions of the Turnmill Street alleys is a disgrace to the parish in which they are situated, and shows something monstrously defective in the working of all the various Acts of Parliaments, passed for the wholesome housing and cleansing of the poor. The houses in the alleys are lofty, each containing ten rooms, and in the majority of cases every room harbours a family. In one of the houses . . . *fifty-six* individuals find shelter, and the rent of the dilapidated, dark, and miserable structure amounts to 26s. a week. "Rents are going up too", a lodger who paid 1s. 9d. for a mite of a room which whitewashed and otherwise rendered decent might serve as a kennel for a mastiff, told me.

An illustration from Greenwood's The Wilds of London *(1874). What are the children doing? Why would it not be allowed today?*

Greenwood's books were interestingly written and often amusing. They were widely read by the middle-classes, making them aware of the lives of those less fortunate than themselves.

Dudley Street, Seven Dials, London. Another illustration from Doré's London *(1872). Why are so many young children out so late at night?*

Can you suggest reasons why the rents were increasing? (Clue: road-widening and railway-building.)

Octavia Hill and Housing the Poor

Octavia Hill was well educated and from a comfortable home. In her twenties she decided to devote her life to improving the housing conditions of the working people many of whom lived in overcrowded, insanitary conditions. She believed that good housing at reasonable rents should be provided but that the tenants must also be prepared to help themselves.

Portrait of Octavia Hill by Sargent. This portrait is owned by the National Trust, of which Octavia Hill was a founder member.

TENANTS NEED HELP

In *The Homes of the London Poor* (1875) Octavia Hill wrote:

> The people's homes are bad partly because they are badly built and arranged, they are ten fold worse because their tenants' habits and lives are what they are. Transplant them tomorrow to healthy and commodious homes, and they would pollute and destroy them. They need, and will need for some time, a reformatory work which will demand that loving zeal of individuals which cannot be had for money, and cannot be legislated for by Parliament.

Why did Octavia Hill believe that providing better housing alone was insufficient? Do you agree with her argument?

THE SOLUTION

The Westminster Review for January 1884 suggested the answer lay in private schemes for the poor, rather than help from the State. It argued that only the sanitary inspectors, landlords and rent collectors could legally enter their homes.

> The former is the tenants' natural enemy; he is the man who burnt their only bed after the baby on it died of scarlet-fever. But the latter may be, and under Miss Hill's system is, their best and kindest friend. It is he, or she, that teaches them to take a pride in being clean and neat themselves, and in keeping the room clean and neat as well. The happiest thing that can happen to the outcasts of London is that they should come under the care of a truly philanthropic [caring] landlord.

Is help of this kind as necessary today? If so, where could it be obtained?

THE SCHEME IN PRACTICE

Octavia Hill described in *The Homes of the London Poor* (1875) how she had begun with three houses in one of the worst parts of Marylebone, London:

> As soon as I entered into possession, each family had an opportunity of doing better; those who would not pay, or who led clearly immoral lives, were ejected. The rooms they vacated were cleansed; the tenants who showed signs of improvement moved into them . . . each room distempered [whitewashed] and painted. The drains were put in order, a large slate cistern was fixed, and the wash house was cleared of its lumber [timber] and thrown open on stated days to each tenant in turn. The roof, the plaster, the woodwork was repaired, the staircase walls were distempered; new grates were fixed, the layers of paper and rag (black with age) were torn from the windows, and glass was put in: out of 192 panes, only eight were unbroken. The yard and footpath were paved.

How had she sought to improve the properties? Do you consider her measures harsh or practical? In her book she stressed that all this could be done and a profit still achieved by the landlord.

A PEN PICTURE

Beatrice Webb's diary entry for 12 May 1886 describes a meeting with Octavia Hill.

> I met Miss Octavia Hill the other night at the Barnetts'. She is a small woman, with large head finely set on her shoulders. The form of her head and features, and the expression of the eyes and mouth, show the attractiveness of mental power. A peculiar charm in her smile. We talked on Artisans' Dwellings. I asked her whether she thought it necessary to keep accurate descriptions of the tenants. No, she did not see the use of it. "Surely it was wise to write down observations so as to be able to give true information?" I suggested. She objected that there was already too much "windy talk". What you wanted was action, for men and women to go and work day by day among the less fortunate. And so there was a slight clash between us, and I felt penitent for my presumption, but *not convinced.*

What is your picture of Octavia Hill from this account? On what point did Beatrice Webb and Octavia Hill disagree?

Sissinghurst in Kent, one of the properties belonging to the National Trust. Octavia Hill's interest in urban problems led her into the Open Space Movement, which resulted in the foundation, in 1895, of the National Trust for Places of Historic Interest and Natural Beauty.

Rowland Hill and the Penny Post

Rowland Hill was an active campaigner. He was involved in various movements such as those for the reform of Parliament, emigration for the poor and the provision of cheap books of quality and information for the people. He is best known for the introduction of the Penny Post, but this came after he was forced to abandon his first career through illness.

THE SCHOOL REFORMER

Rowland Hill's father owned a private boarding school called Hazelwood, near Birmingham, which in time Rowland took over. In 1823 he and his two brothers published plans for the better management of the school.

> The principle of our government is to leave as much as possible all powers in the hands of the boys themselves. To this end we permit them to elect a Committee, which enacts the laws of the school, subject, however, to the veto of the headmaster. We have also courts of justice for the trial of civil and criminal cases and a vigorous police for the preserving of order.

Who do you think formed the "vigorous police"?

Later in the same year Rowland Hill sent a letter to parents:

> Six years have now passed since we placed a great part of the government of the school in the hands of the boys themselves, and during the whole of that time the headmaster has never once executed his right of veto upon their proceedings.

How does this letter bear out the success of Rowland Hill's ideas?

PRESSURE FOR CHANGE

When Rowland Hill gave up teaching he turned his attention to the Post Office, which was badly in need of reform. Postal rates varied according to distance, and the receiver, not the sender, paid the fee. But what concerned Hill most was the cost of postage. In 1837 he published a pamphlet on Post Office reform. It was disliked by the Post Office but taken up by Parliament. In May 1838 a deputation of 150 M.P.s saw the Prime Minister, Lord Melbourne. An Irish member, Daniel O'Connell said

> Consider, my Lord, that a letter to Ireland and the Answer back, would cost thousands upon thousands of my poor and affectionate countrymen considerably more than a fifth of their week's wages. They are too poor to find out secondary conveyances, and if you shut the Post Office to them, which you do now, you shut warm hearts and generous affections from home, kindred [relations], and friends.

Look at the document opposite and see how much a letter to Ireland cost in 1838.

Stamps from Mexico, Portugal and Great Britain commemorating The Penny Post and Rowland Hill. What was our first stamp called?

Eliezer Edwards in *Sir Rowland Hill* (1879) remembers the first day of the Penny Post: 10 January 1840:

On the evening of that day I stood within the hall of the General Post Office, St. Martin's-le-Grand, London. There was a great but orderly crowd. A passage to the letter boxes was kept clear by the police. As the hands of the clock approached the hour of six, the time fixed for closing, the crowd increased. At the first stroke of the clock, the letter boxes were suddenly shut with a sharp ring. There arose from that crowd a shout I shall never forget. It was a shout of victory!

Why does the writer believe this day to be so important?

Postal Rates in Great Britain from Kelly's Post Office London Directory, *1839. Work out the cost of sending a letter from London to Birmingham.*

On 28 August 1879 *The Times* reported Rowland Hill's death. This is part of the obituary:

We can state that about 106 million of chargeable letters and newspapers were sent through the Post Office in 1839 and that 1478 million were sent last year. But the mind cannot grasp such numbers as these. Something more is understood when we are told that in 1839 the average number of letters per head was three and that last year it was 32. . . . We must remember that every civilized country in the world has more or less adopted his plan; that communication has been made so certain, so rapid and so cheap, that the distant traveller, the emigrant – nay even the exile – feels that those whom he has left behind him in his old home are in one way still very near him.

Why does *The Times* believe that the Penny Post was so important? I wonder how many letters you write each year.

IN GREAT BRITAIN.

	Postage of a Single Letter in British Pence.
	d.
FROM any Post Office in England or Wales to any Place not exceeding 15 Miles from such Office . .	4
For any distance above 15 Miles, and not exceeding 20 Miles	5
For any Distance above 20 and not exceeding 30 Miles . .	6
For any Distance above 30 and not exceeding 50 Miles . .	7
For any Distance above 50 and not exceeding 80 Miles . .	8
For any Distance above 80 and not exceeding 120 Miles . .	9
For any Distance above 120 and not exceeding 170 Miles . .	10
For any Distance above 170 and not exceeding 230 Miles . .	11
For any Distance above 230 and not exceeding 300 Miles . .	12

And so in Proportion ; the Postage increasing progressively One Penny for a Single Letter for every like Excess of Distance of 100 Miles.

═════════James Kay-Shuttleworth:═════════

James Kay-Shuttleworth was a doctor by profession and became an Assistant Poor Law Commissioner for the Eastern Counties in 1834. Later he became involved in the development of education. Education in the 1830s was run by the two leading voluntary societies, representing the Church of England (National Society) and the Nonconformists (British and Foreign School Society). The first Government grant was made in 1833 and this was followed by the appointment of inspectors. It was not until the end of the century that education became compulsory and free.

INSTRUCTIONS TO INSPECTORS

In 1839 Kay-Shuttleworth was appointed secretary to the Privy Council concerned with education. One of his first actions was to appoint two inspectors to supervise the government grants which had been made to the two leading voluntary school societies. This extract is taken from his *Instructions to Inspectors* (1840):

> 2. While an important part of these duties will consist of visiting from time to time, schools aided by grants of public money . . . in order to ascertain that the grant has in each case been duly applied, and to enable you to furnish accurate information as to the discipline, management, and methods of instruction pursued in such schools . . . my Lords have in view the encouragement of local efforts for the improvement and extension of elementary education whether made by voluntary associations or by private individuals. The employment of inspectors is therefore intended to advance this object, by affording the promoters of schools, an opportunity of

PUPIL-TEACHERS

Most of the children who attended school had left by their early teens. Thus those intending to teach had several years to wait before they could go to college. To bridge the gap Kay-Shuttleworth invented the pupil-teacher system in 1846. These are excerpts from the regulations:

> **Pupil-Teachers – Qualifications of Candidates . . .**
> **They must be at least 13 years of age, and must not be subject to any bodily infirmity likely to impair their usefulness . . .**
>
> **Candidates will also be required:**
> 1. **To read with fluency, ease and expression.**
> 2. **To write in a neat hand, with correct spelling and punctuation, a simple prose narrative read to them.**
> 3. **To write from dictation sums in the first four rules of arithmetic, simple and compound, to work them correctly, and to know the table of weights and measures.**
> 4. **To point out the parts of speech in a simple sentence.**
> 5. **To have an elementary knowledge of geography.**

> ascertaining, [through] visits of inspection, what improvements in the apparatus and internal arrangement of school, in school management and discipline, and in the methods of teaching [might be made] . . .

List the duties of the inspectors. Why do you think that the Privy Council insisted on inspection once the Government grants had been made?

7. To teach a junior class to the satisfaction of the inspector.
8. Girls should also be able to sew neatly and to knit.

No. 6 concerned the level of religious knowledge required in Church and Chapel schools.

How would you have fared? Do you think that 13 was too young an age to take such responsibility?

The pupil-teachers remained in the school until 18, when they applied to go to a training college.

URBAN AND RURAL CHILDREN

Kay-Shuttleworth wrote many reports based on direct observation. In one, written in the 1840s, he compared the problems presented by urban and rural children. The first excerpt is from the rural manufacturing districts of the West Riding of Yorkshire:

They probably have never lived but in a hovel, have never been in a street of a village or a town; are unacquainted with common usages of social life; probably never saw a book; are bewildered by the rapid motion of crowds; confused in an assemblage of scholars. They have to be taught to stand upright – to walk without a slouching gait – to sit without crouching like a sheepdog. They have to learn some decency in their skin, hair and dress. They are commonly either cowed, and sullen or wild, fierce and obstinate.

The second is from the East End of London:

A different kind of brutishness is shown by a large class of scholars living in the most degraded parts of great cities. A London child, living in a street of brothels and thieves' dens with parents living abandoned lives, spends his days in the kennel among sharp-witted restless little creatures like himself. He is his own master. His powers of observation are particularly acute; his power of decision rapid, his will energetic . . . . Perhaps he is an accomplished thief or beggar, or picks up a precarious living by holding horses, sweeping a crossing or costermongering [street-selling].

How do you account for the great differences between the urban and rural child? Would you have preferred to be a pupil-teacher in a town or in the country?

It was not until the end of the century that education became compulsory and free but Sir Michael Sadler considered that Kay-Shuttleworth had played an important part: "To him more than to anyone else we owe it that England is supplied with schools for the children of the people."

Dinner at Hanwell District School in the 1870s. These schools were for pauper children from a number of unions and were favoured by Kay-Shuttleworth. They were intended to instil order and discipline.

Charles Kingsley: a Christian Socialist

Charles Kingsley was one of the founders of Christian Socialism. He himself was a minister in the Church of England and his strong belief in social reform was expressed through his novels and pamphlets.

SWEATSHOPS

In 1850 Charles Kingsley published a pamphlet *Cheap Clothes and Nasty* under the pseudonym of Parson Lot. He had been inspired by the recent articles of Henry Mayhew in the *Morning Chronicle* which had investigated the sweatshops in the London clothing industry. Charles Kingsley quoted one worker as saying,

> **One sweater I worked with had four children and six men, and they, together with his wife, sister-in-law, and himself, all lived in two rooms, the largest of which was about eight feet by ten. We worked in the smallest room and slept there as well – all six of us. There were two turn-up beds in it, and we slept three in a bed. There was no chimney, and indeed, no ventilation whatever. I was near losing my life there – the foul air of so many people working all day in the place, and sleeping there at night, was quite suffocating. Almost all the men were consumptive, and I myself attended the dispensary for disease of the lungs .... We were all sick and weak and loth to work.**

For this accommodation each worker paid 2s. 6d. a week rent. Why were these conditions such a danger to health?

Linley Sambourne illustration in Punch *(1888).* ▶
What point is he trying to make? How effective is he?

ALTON LOCKE: TAILOR AND POET

In the same year, 1850, Charles Kingsley used the material he had gathered in the novel *Alton Locke*. Alton was a small London tradesman and in this extract he describes being taken to a London slum by a clergyman.

> **We went through a back street or two, and then into a huge, miserable house, which a hundred years ago, perhaps, had witnessed the luxury, and rung to the laughter of some new great fashionable family, alone there in their glory. Now every room of it held its family, or its group of families . . . its grand staircase, with the carved balustrades rotting and crumbling away piecemeal, converted into a common sewer for all its inmates. Up**

THE SWEATER'S FURNACE: OR, THE REAL "CURSE" OF LABOUR

stair after stair we went, while wails of children, and curses of men, steamed out upon the hot stifling rush of air from every doorway, till at the topmost story, we knocked at a garret door. We entered.

Why was this large old house now divided up between poor families? Imagine you were with Alton Locke and the clergyman. Write a paragraph describing what you found when you entered the room.

THE BAD SQUIRE

In *Yeast*, serialized in *Frazer's Magazine* in 1847, and published as a novel in 1850, Kingsley's Cornish gamekeeper, Tregarva, wrote the following poem:

You have sold the labouring-men,
   squire.
Body and soul to shame,
To pay for your seat in the House,
   squire.
And to pay for the feed of your game.

You made him a poacher yourself,
   squire,
When you'd give neither work nor
   meat,
And your barley-fed hares robbed the
   garden
At our starving children's feet.
When, packed in one reeking chamber,
Man, maid, mother, and little ones lay:
While the rain pattered in on the rotting
   bride-bed,
And the walls let in the day;
When we lay in the burning fever.

CHOLERA IN CORNWALL

In *Two Years Ago* (1857) Charles Kingsley takes up the cause of public health. His heroine in *Yeast* had died of typhus; in this novel the disease is cholera. The young new doctor in the village had warned of the outbreak but he was rebuked by his senior partner.

"And what be you thinking of, sir, to expect me to offend all my best patients? And not one of 'em but rents some two cottages, some a dozen. And what'll they say to me if I go a routing and rookling in their drains, like an old sow by the wayside, besides putting 'em to all manner of expense? And all on the chance of this cholera coming, which I have no faith in, nor in this new-fangled sanitary reform neither, which is all a dodge for a lot of young Government puppies to fill their pockets, and rule and ride over us."

Why is the young doctor urged to do nothing? Compare this evidence with that of Edwin Chadwick. How does Kingsley aid the work of Chadwick?

One of Charles Kingsley's books has been turned into a film. Do you know what it is called? (Clue: one of the characters is a chimney-sweep.)

On the mud of the cold clay floor,
   Till you parted us all for three months,
   squire;
At the cursed workhouse door.

In the last verse the family are ill. In what other ways does Kingsley suggest that the squire acted cruelly?

Henry Mayhew: a Reforming Journalist

Henry Mayhew was a journalist who helped found the humorous magazine *Punch* in 1841. Unfortunately, by 1847 he was bankrupt and in the following year he took a job as a reporter with the *Morning Chronicle*, a reforming newspaper.

A VISIT TO THE CHOLERA DISTRICTS OF BERMONDSEY

On 24 September 1847 the *Morning Chronicle* carried an unsigned article by Mayhew in which he described the notorious Jacob's Island.

> We then journeyed on to London-street, down which the tidal ditch continues its course. In No. 1 of this street the cholera first appeared seventeen years ago, and spread up it with fearful virulence; but this year it appeared at the opposite end, and ran down it with like severity. As we passed along the reeking banks of the sewer the sun shone upon a narrow slip of the water. In the bright light it appeared the colour of strong green tea, and positively looked as solid as black marble in the shadow – indeed it was more like watery mud than muddy water; and yet we were assured this was the only water the wretched inhabitants had to drink. As we gazed in horror at it, we saw drains and sewers emptying their filthy contents into it; we saw a whole tier of doorless privies [lavatories] in the open road, common to men and women, built over it; we heard bucket after bucket of filth splash into it, and the limbs of the vagrant boys bathing in it seemed by pure force of contrast, white as Parian marble . . .

How does this type of writing help the cause of public health reform? After this Mayhew wrote twice-weekly letters for the paper based upon his observations and interviews.

CHILDREN AS CHEAP LABOUR

In Letter XXXII (4 February 1850) Mayhew aimed to let the people tell their own story. How effective a technique do you think this is? Here, a shoemaker tells of his problems.

> "A man's own children will soon be the means of driving him from the market altogether, or compelling him to come down to their rate of wages; and if we are forced to put our children to work directly they are able, they cannot receive any education whatever, and then their minds and bodies will be both stunted. Of course, that must have a demoralizing effect upon the next generation. For my own part, as the trade is going down every day, I could not think of bringing my boys to it [shoemaking], considering their future welfare – and what else I am to do with them I can't say. My earnings are so small now and my income so much reduced, that I shouldn't have the means to apprentice them to any other trade . . . ."

This illustration is taken from Mayhew's London Labour and the London Poor. *What are these people doing on the refuse heap and why are the children in the foreground?*

A POOR TAILOR

Mayhew was particularly concerned with the plight of the London tailors. In 1850 he wrote:

> A card was put into my hands on my rounds: it ran as follows:
>
> to be raffled
> on Monday the 17th of December at the Angel & crown, ship alley, Wellclose sqre.
> A WAISTCOAT
> the property of W.W., who has had a Long fit of Sickness.
> Chairman Mr. J.F. – Dep. Mr. P.C.
>
> Tickets 6d. Each   Music provided

> I lost no time in seeking out the sick man and found him truly destitute. I was directed to one of the back streets of the Commercial-road; and there, in a small, close, and bare, unfurnished room, stretched on a bed scantily covered, I found the poor sick slop-worker.

The article then went on to describe the condition of the old man. How had Mayhew sought to win the sympathy of his readers?

THE HAM-SANDWICH-SELLER

In October 1850 Mayhew finished with the *Morning Chronicle* and began work on *London Labour and the London Poor,* which was published in 1851. Here he describes one of the many street-traders:

> "Ah, sir! I live very poorly. A ha'prth or a penn'orth of cheap fish, which I cook myself, is one of my treats – either herring or plaice – with a tatur, perhaps. Then there's a sort of meal, now and then, off the odds and ends of the ham, such as isn't quite viewy enough for the public, along with the odds and ends of the loaves .... A man that sometimes makes only 3s. 6d. a week, and sometimes less, and must pay 2s. rent out of that, must look after every farthing. I've often walked eight miles to see if I could find ham a halfpenny a pound cheaper elsewhere .... If I was sick there's only the parish for me."

What is so disturbing about the amount paid in rent?

The cover of one of Mayhew's part magazines. Why do you think he sold them in this form? ▼

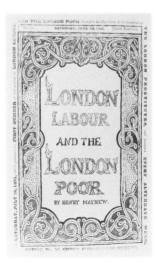

Florence Nightingale

Nursing in the early Victorian period was at a very low ebb. Nurses had no real training and were looked down on by society. Florence Nightingale helped to transform nursing into the respected profession that it is today. Her first opportunity came when she was made superintendent of a sanitorium for sick governesses in Harley Street in August 1853. She soon established a reputation for firm organization, especially during the cholera outbreak in the summer of 1854.

RUSSELL'S DESPATCH FROM THE CRIMEA

In March 1854 the British and the French went to war with Russia. The war was largely fought in Southern Russia, in the Crimea. The wounded were cared for across the Black Sea in the Turkish town of Scutari. It was from there *The Times* war correspondent, William Russell, reported on the appalling conditions in the hospital at Scutari. In a despatch on 9 October 1854 he wrote:

> **It is with feelings of surprise and anger that the public will learn that no sufficient preparations have been made for the care of the wounded. Not only are there not sufficient surgeons . . . there is not even linen to make bandages . . . there is no preparation for the commonest surgical operation! Not only are the men kept, in some cases for a week, without the hand of a medical man coming near their wounds, not only are they left to expire in agony . . . and that men must die through the medical staff of the British Army having forgotten that old rags are necessary for the dressing of wounds.**

What were Russell's main criticisms? What would their impact have been?

CALLED TO SERVICE

Russell's despatches created a scandal at home. *The Times* established a fund to raise money to send 40 nurses to Scutari and on 15 October 1854 Sidney Herbert, the Minister of War, formally invited Florence Nightingale to be in charge:

THE CONDITIONS AT SCUTARI

Mr Augustus Stafford, M.P., visited Scutari in 1854. These are extracts from evidence that he gave to the Roebuck Committee in 1855 on conditions of the British troops. The scandal brought down the government.

> **Everyone helped, the official people were assisting as much as possible but the number of official people were too small and the arrival was so great, a flood of sick came upon them, bursting in so suddenly that the means of the hospital were not able to meet it . . . . The majority of the cases at the Barrack Hospital were suffering from diarrhoea, they had no slippers and no shoes, and they had to go into this filth so that gradually they did not go into the lavatory chamber itself.**

Cecil Woodham-Smith in *Florence Nightingale* (1950) quotes one of her letters home:

> **. . . the dysentery cases have died at the rate of one in two . . . the mortality of the operations is frightful . . . . This is only the beginning of things.**

Why is it useful to the historian to find two similar eye-witness reports?

32

and the Nursing Profession

Dear Miss Nightingale,

You will have seen in the papers that there is a great deficiency of nurses at the Hospital at Scutari.

. . . My question simply is, would you listen to the request to go and superintend the whole thing? You would of course have plenary [complete] authority over all the nurses . . . deriving your authority from the Government, your position would secure the respect and consideration of every one.

. . . I know you will come to a wise decision. God grant it may be in accordance with my hopes!

Believe me dear Miss Nightingale,

Ever yours

Sidney Herbert

Florence accepted, but who might have been resentful of her authority in Scutari?

A contemporary print showing the ward in the Scutari Hospital. How many improvements can you identify?

ACTION TAKEN

Florence Nightingale's presence and help was, in time, accepted. In a letter of 14 December 1854 to Sir Sidney Herbert she wrote:

What we may be considered as having effected:
1. The kitchen for extra diets now in full action.
2. A great deal more cleaning of wards, mops, scrubbing brushes, brooms and combs given out by ourselves.
3. 2000 shoes, cotton and flannel given out and washing organized.
4. Lying-in hospital begun.
5. Widows and soldiers. Wives relieved and attended to.
6. A great amount of daily dressing and attention to compound fractures by the most competent of us.
7. The supervision and stirring-up of the whole machinery generally with the concurrance of the chief medical authority.
8. The repairing of wards for 800 wounded which would otherwise have been left uninhabitable. (And this I regard as the most important.)

Why do you think that she regarded number 8 as the most important achievement?

Florence Nightingale once said "The first aim of a hospital should be to do the sick no harm." Why do you think that her work at Scutari was so important for both the future of nursing and hospitals in general? When Florence Nightingale returned to England she set up the Nightingale Training School, which raised the skill and status of the nurse by providing a professional training.

Seebohm Rowntree and Poverty in York

Seebohm Rowntree was inspired by Charles Booth's *Life and Labour of the People in London* to conduct a similar survey of York, to find the degree of poverty in that city. The survey was conducted in 1899 and covered 11,560 families and 388 streets (i.e. 46,754 people).

THE CITY OF YORK

York was, and is, regarded as a great tourist attraction. Black's *Guide to the County of York* (1894) described it thus:

> **No city in the Empire can boast of an antiquity greater or more celebrated than that of York . . . . York is situated . . . in one of the richest and most extensive vales in England . . . . There are iron-foundries, and an extensive glass manufacturing. Brewing and comb-making are extensively carried on . . . . York has much of the life and activity of the present and seems to hold out the promise of advancing in importance and material wealth.**

AN OFFICE CLEANER'S BUDGET

Rowntree and his researchers constructed a detailed description of the home, work, and the way each family spent its money. In *Poverty: A Study of Town Life* (1901) he described an office cleaner and her daughter, whose wages were irregular but who, between them, during a four-week period, averaged 11s. 9d. per week:

> **Mother and daughter live in one room, for which they pay 1/8d. per week rent. It is three storeys up, and is approached by a crooked, narrow, wooden staircase which is unventilated, and almost pitch dark.**

The room was well kept and spotlessly clean, however.

This hardly seemed a city where much poverty would be found.

Rowntree was able to send visitors to study the majority of York's families. Why was he able to conduct a far more extensive survey than Booth?

No. 1 STREET.

PRIMARY AND SECONDARY POVERTY

On the evidence of the information collected, Rowntree concluded that one could divide the poor into two categories:

a. Families whose total earnings were insufficient to obtain the minimum necessaries for the maintenance of merely physical efficiency. Poverty falling under this head was described as "primary" poverty.

b. Families whose total earnings would have been sufficient for the maintenance of merely physical efficiency were it not that some portion of it was absorbed by other expenditure, either useful or wasteful. Poverty falling under this head was described as "secondary" poverty.

The percentages falling into each group were:

		Proportion of total population of York
Persons in "primary" poverty	7,230	9.91%
Persons in "secondary" poverty	13,072	17.93%
Total number of persons living in poverty	20,302	27.84%

Charles Booth had found that 30.7 per cent of those living in London were living in poverty. Why, then do you think that Rowntree's figures caused such surprise and concern?

WHY PEOPLE ARE POOR

Rowntree detailed the causes of poverty as follows:

a. **Immediate causes of "primary" poverty**
1. **Death of chief wage-earner.**
2. **Incapacity of chief wage-earner through accident, illness, or old age.**
3. **Chief wage-earner out of work.**
4. **Chronic irregularity of work (sometimes due to incapacity or unwillingness of worker to undertake regular employment).**
5. **Largeness of family, i.e. cases in which the family is in poverty because there are more than four children, though it would not have been in poverty had the number of children not exceeded four.**
6. **Lowness of wage, i.e. where the chief wage-earner is in regular work, but at wages which are insufficient to maintain a moderate family (i.e. not more than four children) in a state of physical efficiency.**
b. **Immediate causes of "secondary" poverty**
   Drink, betting and gambling. Ignorant or careless housekeeping, and other improvident [unwise] expenditure, the latter often induced by irregularity of income.

What do you think were the major causes of primary poverty? Are there any means by which secondary poverty can be helped?

◀ *Part of the detail from No. 1 Street (name kept secret). Work through each line and decide which were the two poorest families.*

Titus Salt and Saltaire

Titus Salt was a successful woollen manufacturer. He had a factory in Bradford, where he was Mayor in 1848-9. At the height of his fame it was said that he made a £1000 each day before the ordinary person got out of bed. He was the first to use donskoi and alpaca wool. Titus Salt is a good example of a highly successful businessman who was also a model employer.

A VIEW OF BRADFORD

In the second quarter of the nineteenth century Bradford became the leading worsted textile city, and many new factories were built as the population increased two and a half times. George Weerth, a German writer, lived in Bradford in the 1840s.

> Every other factory town in England is a paradise in comparison to this hole. In Manchester the air lies like lead upon you; in Birmingham it is just as if you were sitting with your nose in a stove pipe; in Leeds you have to cough with the dust and the stink as if you had swallowed a pound of Cayenne pepper at one go – but you can still put up with all that. In Bradford however, you think you have been lodged with the Devil incarnate . . . . If anyone wants to feel how a poor sinner is perhaps tormented in Purgatory, let him travel to Bradford. (Quoted in J. Reynolds, *Saltaire*, 1976)

Can you think why Bradford was so bad, in terms of housing and smoke?

SALTAIRE

Titus Salt decided to build a new factory three miles outside Bradford. He called it Saltaire. In Cassell's

Illustrated History of England (c. 1870s) Sir W. Fairbairn wrote:

> The Saltaire mills are situated in one of the most beautiful parts of the romantic valley of the Aire. The site has been selected with uncommon judgement . . . The estate is bounded by highways and railways which penetrate to the very centre of the buildings, and is intersected by both canal and river. Admirable water is obtained for the use of the steam-engines and for the different processes of the manufacture. By the distance of the mills from the smoky and cloudy atmosphere of a large town an unobstructed and good light is secured; whilst, both by land and water, direct communication is gained for the importance of coal and all other raw produce . . . and for the exportation and delivery of manufactured goods . . .

Why does the author think that the site was particularly well chosen?

An illustration of Saltaire in the 1870s. Try and match it up with the plan.

THE SCHOOL

Titus Salt set out to build a model town not only for his workers, but also for their families. It was commenced in 1851 and completed during the next 20 years. George Bartley in *The Schools for the People* (1871) described the school which Salt had built:

> **Description of Buildings** – These are subdivided as usual, for Infants, Girls and Boys. Each class of children has a separate Schoolroom, to which is attached the necessary class-rooms. There is also a large playground, and a covered recreation-shed for wet weather .... In 1869, Mr Fitch, in his Report, stated that the Saltaire Boys' School was rapidly becoming one of the best, as it was already the handsomest, schools in his district.

Locate the school on the accompanying map. In 1870 1010 children attended the school.

A MODEL TOWN

In 1876 J.M. Wilson described Saltaire in *The Imperial Gazeteer of England and Wales*:

> **Consists of well-planned streets, it is generally regarded as a model town; underwent great enlargement in 1866-8; contains a great factory built in 1853, and another built in 1865; and has a railway station, good shops, a public newsroom and library, gas-works, wash-houses, schools and Independent and Wesylon chapels, and 40 alms-houses . . . a public park was formed in 1870. Population in 1868, about 5,000.**

The Times obituary for Titus Salt, on 30 December 1876, stated that married couples in the almshouses received 10s. per week, the unmarried 7s. 6d.

All the features mentioned in the extract are shown on the map. How can you tell that Saltaire has been planned?

A plan of Saltaire taken from Bartley's The Schools for the People *(1871). Link this with the written description.*

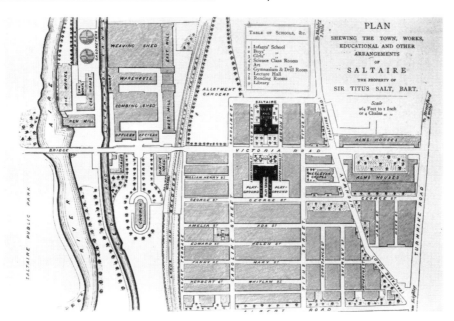

37

The Earl of Shaftesbury:

For many years, until 1857, Anthony Ashley Cooper was a member of the House of Commons. In that year, on the death of his father, he became the Earl of Shaftesbury and took his place in the House of Lords. Throughout his life he worked for reform. In 1848 he said: "It will involve trouble, anxiety, reproach, abuse, unpopularity; I shall became a target for private assault and the public press."

WOMEN AND CHILDREN IN THE MINES

As an M.P. Shaftesbury was responsible for Parliament setting up a Children's Employment Commission to investigate a wide range of child labour. In its first Report, in 1842, it outlined the conditions of children working in the coal mines. This enabled Shaftesbury to put a Mines Bill before the House of Commons in 1842. His two-hour speech before the House was reprinted in *Speeches of the Earl of Shaftesbury* (1868):

> **The child, it appears, has a girdle round its waist, to which is attached a chain, which passes under the legs, and is attached to the cart. The child is obliged to pass on all fours . . . . This kind of labour they have to continue during several hours in a temperature described as perfectly intolerable . . . it appears that the girdle blisters their sides and causes great pain . . . . In the West Riding, it appears, girls are almost universally employed as trappers and hurriers, in common with the boys. The girls are of all ages, from 7 to 21.**

The Bill was successful and the Mines Act of 1842 forbade the employment of women, girls, and boys under 10 underground in mines.

RAGGED SCHOOLS

In 1846 Shaftesbury was the person largely responsible for founding the Ragged School Union of which he became President. Its work was described in a special supplement to *The Graphic* in October 1885:

> **The first inmates of the schools were more than ordinarily rough, and the teacher's work was not a little dangerous. In fifteen schools there were 2,345 children. Of these 162 confessed that they had been in prison; 116 had run away from their homes; 170 slept in lodging-houses – and the lodging-houses then were perfect dens of crime; 253 lived by begging; 216 had no shoes and stockings; 280 had no hat, cap, or bonnet; 101 had no body linen; 249 had never slept in beds; 68 were the children of convicts; and 306 had lost one or both parents.**

Why do you think that Shaftesbury believed that these children should go to school?

Doré's illustration of a scripture reader in a night refuge. People like Shaftesbury who took the Christian message to the people were called evangelicals. What is the form of lighting?

a Reforming Peer

In a speech made at St George's Hall in Liverpool on 12 October 1858 Shaftesbury, after describing the appalling conditions that he had seen in the slums, said:

> **If you find them covered with vermin [and I must say I have gone amongst them with my friends; and have returned . . . with a considerable household of vermin upon my back] – if you go and see these things do not lay the blame upon them, but upon yourselves. You have knowledge, you have means. They have not knowledge, they have not means; and by everything true, by everything holy, you are your brother's keeper.**

Why did Shaftesbury believe that the educated must help the poor, and that the poor could only improve through education? Do you think he was right?

Shaftesbury died on 2 October 1885 and the *Spectator* paid this tribute:

> **A noble life ended on Thursday, when Lord Shaftesbury died at Folkestone. He was one of the very few men of whom it is easy to say with certainty that the world was the better because he lived. There are literally hundreds of thousands in England who are today directly happier and better for his work. A Peer of historic rank, with an adequate fortune, and the road to power fully open to him, he devoted himself for 50 years to the amelioration [improvement]of the condition of the oppressed . . . . It was mainly owing to his exertions that the Factory Acts were passed, and that the system of slavery for women and children which reigned in British coalmines, and the horrors of which this generation would not believe, was finally brought to an end. He carried the Truck Act and the Ten Hours' Bill; he freed the wretched children apprenticed to the sweeps; and he was the founder and mainspring of the Ragged Schools, out of which the demand for national education originally sprang.**

What did the writer believe were his major achievements? Try and find out what the Truck Act and the Ten Hour Bill were.

◀ *An illustration from Mayhew's* London Labour and the London Poor *(1851). Shaftesbury was responsible for the Climbing Boys Act of 1875 which forbade child sweeps.*

Beatrice Webb

Beatrice Potter (in 1892 she married Sidney Webb) spent her long life concerned with many social and economic problems, ranging from sweated labour to casual labour in the docks. She worked for both Octavia Hill in the Charity Organization Society and Charles Booth on his survey.

COMMENT ON HENRY MAYHEW

Beatrice Webb kept a detailed diary throughout her life. This was used extensively in her autobiography *My Apprenticeship* (1926). Since its publication the diary itself has been published. This extract comes from the entry for 22 August 1887:

> **Mayhew's *London Life and Labour* (1851) is good material spoilt by bad dressing. It is a mine of observation and of statistical enquiry, but there is no opening to it, nor any destination reached. It is overloaded with descriptive detail.** (N. and J. Mackenzie, *The Diary of Beatrice Webb*, Vol. I, 1982)

Beatrice had decided that she was going to be a social investigator. In what ways does she intend to differ from Henry Mayhew?

Why did Punch *produce this cartoon in 1888?*

THE MODERN VENUS ATTIRED BY THE THREE DIS-GRACES.

THE DOCKS

Her diary contains interesting insights into many different situations. The entry for 12 May 1887 describes a visit to the London Docks:

> **Docks early morning. Permanent men respectable and clean. Casuals low-looking – bestial, content with their own condition. Brutal fight and struggle. (As a few men are given work for the day.) Sudden dissolution of the crowd, with coarse jokes and loud laugh. Look of utter indifference on their faces. Among them are one or two who have fallen from better things. Abject misery and hopeless determination to struggle on. The mass of rejected lounge down to another dock or spread over the entrances to the various wharves . . . . Some hundred of the lowest will congregate, waiting on the chance of a foreman needing an odd man.**

and the Sweated Industries

BEFORE A SELECT COMMITTEE

Beatrice became an expert on the sweated industries and thus, when a House of Lords Select Committee was established to report on the *Sweating Industry in the East End* (1888), she was called as a witness on 11 May, 1888:

> **Chairman. You have had some considerable experience, have you not, in the East-End of London? And from your personal experience you know a good deal about what is commonly called the sweating system?**
> **– In the tailoring trade, but only in the tailoring trade.**
> **How would you define the sweating system?**
> **– I should say that an inquiry into the sweating system was practically an inquiry into all labour employed in manufacture which had escaped the regulation of the Factory Act and trade unions.**
> **. . . What are the hours?**
> **The hours for women are of course factory hours; but then in the very lowest class, the shop trade, the employers do not pay very much attention to that, and they work from 8 or 7 half-past in the morning till 10 or 11 at night.**

What would have been the benefit of applying the Factory Acts to the sweated industries? Do you think the absence of trade unions harmed the worker?

Can you work out what a casual dock labourer does from this description? Why did Beatrice Webb believe that the system helped to make the men what they were?

A TWELVE-HOUR DAY

In October 1888 she contributed an article, entitled "Pages from a Workgirl's Diary", to *The Nineteenth Century*, a radical, middle-class journal. These were drawn from her experiences as a worker among the garment workers of the East End of London. She had learnt to sew and took the job in a typical sweatshop in order to write the article.

> **Some thirty women and girls are crowding in . . . . There is a general Babel of voices as each "hand" settles down in front of the bundle of work and the old tobacco or candlebox that holds the cottons, twist, gimp, needles, thimbles, and scissors belonging to her. They are all English or Irish women, with the exception of some half dozen well-dressed "young ladies" (daughters of the house) one of whom acts as forewoman . . .**

Twelve hours later:

> **"Eight o'clock by the Brewery clock", cries the shrill voice. Ten minutes to, shouts the missus, looking at her watch. "However, it ain't worth breaking the law for a few minutes. Stop work."**
> **This is most welcome to me. The heat since the gas has been lit is terrific, my fingers are horribly sore, and my back aches as if it would break . . . outside, the freshness of the evening air, the sensation of free movement, and rest to the weary eyes and fingers constitute the keenest physical enjoyment I have ever yet experienced.**

What do you think was the major advantage of Beatrice experiencing this sort of work for herself? (No one knew that she was not a genuine worker.)

Changes 1837-1901

At the close of Victoria's reign there was still much to be done, as Rowntree's survey showed. Equally, some 25 per cent of those who volunteered to fight for Britain in the Second Boer War (1899-1902) were unfit for military service. Nevertheless, improvements had been considerable and the Liberal Government that came to power in 1906 was to introduce many of the Acts that the reformers had hoped for.

THE GROWTH OF EDUCATION

Sir Herbert Maxwell in *Sixty Years a Queen* (1897), published to commemorate Victoria's Diamond Jubilee, looked at the effects of education:

> **A generation has grown up under universal compulsory education, and it is possible already to calculate some of the effects of that far-reaching measure on the material prosperity, moral character, and literary habits of our people. In regard to the first two, statistics go to show that, notwithstanding an increase of nearly 35% in the population since the introduction of compulsory education in 1871, there had been a decrease between that year and 1894 of nearly 25% in the number of paupers from 1,079,391 to 812,441. The convictions for crime showed a corresponding diminution from 12,953 to 9,634 or rather more than 25%; while during a similar period, the number of "juvenile offenders" has been reduced to the enormous extent of over 71½%.**

Why does the author see a link between increased education and a fall in crime and poverty?

The written word is not always correct, even though it may be a primary source. Check to see whether compulsory education was introduced in 1871.

A Labour Exchange established by the Salvation Army (1890) some 20 years before they were introduced by Parliament. In one year they found work for 16,000 unemployed.

Vaccination against smallpox in a London printing work (c. 1905). Can you identify the two nurses in attendance?

A MORE CONCERNED PEOPLE

Mary Bateson, writing in *Social England* (1897), believed that people were more understanding:

> All classes know each other better now; the arrogance of the aristocracy is less insolent, the bitterness of the democracy [people] less uninformed and ignorant. It is no longer in "contests with the clods" that rich men and poor have their one opportunity of meeting on equal terms. In every large town now there are many who take to heart the existence of an "East End", who are concerned with the problem of the social duties of the rich to the poor, and of who realise something of the difficulties of philanthropy; where formerly it was possible to number the more energetic philanthropists, now their name is legion [many].

To what extent, do you think, were the individuals mentioned in this book responsible for bringing about this closer understanding?

IMPROVED PUBLIC HEALTH

Mary Bateson also wrote of the battle against disease.

> The steady decline of typhus even to a vanishing point is one of the most satisfactory results which has to be recorded in connection with the public health of the last twenty years. The diminution of this disease appears to be the direct outcome of the improved sanitary conditions, under which the

OVERCROWDING

There had been many improvements, but much still remained to be done. Seebohm Rowntree makes this point in the conclusion to *Poverty: A Study of Town Life* (1901):

> *Housing.* It has been shown that in York 4705 persons, or 6.4% of the total population are living more than two persons to a room, whilst the actual number who are living, and especially sleeping, in rooms which provide inadequate air space for the maintenance of health is indoubtedly very much greater. Moreover, the impossibility of maintaining the decencies of life in these overcrowded houses is a factor which cannot fail to affect the morals of their inhabitants.

Why did Rowntree see overcrowding as such a problem?

> poorer classes are living and to the higher standards of comfort which they now demand. Smallpox, like typhus, also appears to be a waning disease. . . . The practice of vaccination was rendered compulsory in 1853, and it became uniform after 1865, when an organized inspection was established throughout the country, and was conducted by officers placed under the control of the Privy Council and afterwards of the Local Government Board.

Which of the reformers mentioned in this book did most to bring about a changing attitude to public health?

alpaca animal similar to a llama with long silken wool.

Artisans' Dwelling Act (1875) Act which gave local authorities permission to demolish slum areas.

casual labourer a worker without fixed employment.

chandler's shop a shop which sells candles, oil or soap, *or* a general dealer.

Cheap Jack a travelling hawker or salesman.

cholera an infectious and deadly disease. Visited Britain in 1831, 1848-9, 1854 and 1866.

Christian Socialism a mid-nineteenth-century movement for applying Christian values to social reform.

consumption a wasting disease.

Crimean War a war fought mainly in Southern Russia and the Black Sea coast between Russia and Britain, France and Piedmont (1854-6).

crossing-sweeper one who cleared a path across the roads in the time of horse-drawn traffic.

dispensary where medicines are given or dispensed.

dividend the interest paid annually to those with shares.

donskoi a wool imported from Russia and first used by Titus Salt.

evangelist one who preaches and takes religion to the people.

Fabian one who believes in the gradual spread of socialism (Fabian Society founded 1884).

gimp a yarn with a hard core.

gin palace a public house.

libel a written accusation.

monopoly exclusive control of the market supply of a product or service.

municipal relating to the government of a town.

obituary article recording a person's death.

pauper a person receiving help from the Poor Rate.

philanthropic doing good for others.

piece-worker person who is paid by how much he or she does, rather than being paid an hourly rate.

Pledge a solemn promise not to drink.

Poor Law Union a group of parishes formed together after the 1834 Act to supervise the poor in their area.

Privy Council an advisory committee of government.

protective tariffs duties or taxes on imports to protect home industries.

radical one who favours considerable reform.

Ragged school voluntary school for destitute children.

Roebuck Committee enquiry into the state of the British army in 1855.

sanitary inspector a health inspector who ensures that the bye-laws are enforced.

slop trade where cheap clothing is made often in sweatshops.

smallpox a contagious feverish disease.

Social Democrats (SDF) a Marxist group formed in Britain in the 1880s.

sweated labour where one works long hours for low wages at home or in unhealthy rooms outside the Factory Acts.

Temperance Society group which campaigns against the abuse of alcoholic drink. Members used to sign the Pledge. Often associated with Church or Chapel.

typhus a dangerous fever which is often transmitted by lice.

worsted a fine woollen fabric.

veto the power of rejecting by saying or voting no.

Book List

Bailey, V. and Wise, E., *Victorian Times* (Longman)

Delgado, A., *Then and There: A Hundred Years of Medical Care* (Longman)

Favell, C., *At the Time of Charles Dickens* (Longman)

Gibson, J., *Chadwick and Shaftesbury* (Methuen)

Harris, S., *Past into Present: Women at Work* (Batsford)

Kent, G., *Past into Present: Poverty* (Batsford)

Jones, M.V., *Finding Out About Industrial Britain; Finding Out About The Poor in Nineteenth-Century Britain* (Batsford)

Longmate, E., *Then and There: Children at Work, 1830-1885* (Longman)

Middleton, G., *The Factory Age* (Longman)

Rawcliffe, J.M., *Finding Out About Victorian Towns; Finding Out About Victorian London; Finding Out About Victorian Public Health and Housing* (Batsford)

Searby, P., *Then and There: Weavers and Outworkers in Victorian Times* (Longman)

Speed, P.F., *Then and There: Learning and Teaching in Victorian Times* (Longman)

Tonge, N. and Quincey, M., *Cholera and Public Health* (Macmillan)

Watson R., *Edwin Chadwick Poor Law and Public Health* (Longman)

Williams-Ellis and Stobbs, W., *Victorian England* (Blackie)

Date List

1837 (June) Death of William IV. Queen Victoria comes to throne.
1838 Charles Dicken's *Oliver Twist*.
Octavia Hill born (d. 1912).
1839 Kay-Shuttleworth appointed secretary to Privy Council of Education.
1840 Kay-Shuttleworth issues instructions to inspectors.
Rowland Hill introduces The Penny Post.
Charles Booth born (d. 1916).
1841 First issue of *Punch*.
1842 Lord Ashley's Mines Act prevents women and children under 10 working underground.
Report by Edwin Chadwick on *The Sanitary Condition of the Labouring Population*.
1844 Factory Act – 12-hour day for women, 6½ hours for 8-13 year-olds.
Royal Commission on the Health of Towns.
1845 Dr Barnardo born (d. 1905).
1846 Repeal of the Corn Laws by Robert Peel.
Daily News founded – first cheap newspaper; Dickens editor.
Pupil-teacher system introduced by Kay-Shuttleworth.
1847 Annie Besant born (d. 1933).
Factory Act – 10-hour day for women and children 13-18.
Charles Dickens's *Dombey and Son*.
Charles Kingsley's *Yeast*.
1848 Public Health Act – local boards of health permitted.
1848-9 Titus Salt Mayor of Bradford.
1849 Charles Kingsley's *Alton Locke*.
1851 Henry Mayhew's *London Labour and London Poor*.
Great Exhibition opens in Hyde Park.
Titus Salt begins building Saltaire.
Isaac Singer invents the sewing machine.
1852 James Greenwood born (d. 1929).
Charles Dickens's *Bleak House*.
1854-6 Crimean War – Florence Nightingale to Scutari.
1857 On death of his father Lord Ashley becomes Earl of Shaftesbury.
Charles Kingsley's *Two Years Ago*.
1848 Beatrice Webb (née Potter) born (d. 1943).
1861 Death of Albert, the Prince Consort.
1863 Charles Kingsley's *The Water Babies*.
1864 Octavia Hill begins reform of tenement dwellings in St Marylebone.
1865 William Booth begins his Christian work amongst the poor.
1866 Dr Barnardo opens home for homeless boys in Stepney.
1870 Education Act establishes board schools.
Death of Charles Dickens.
1871 Seebohm Rowntree born (d. 1954).
1873-6 Joseph Chamberlain Mayor of Birmingham.
1874 James Greenwood's *The Wilds of London*.
1875 Artisans' Dwelling Act.
Octavia Hill's *Homes of the London Poor*.
Charles Kingsley dies.
1876 Dr Barnardo opens home for girls at Barkingside, Essex.
Titus Salt dies.
Joseph Chamberlain enters Parliament.
1877 Kay-Shuttleworth dies.
1878 William Booth founds the Salvation Army.
1879 Rowland Hill dies.
1885 Earl of Shaftesbury dies.
1887 Henry Mayhew dies.
1888 Match girls strike at Bryant and May's factory. Beatrice Webb takes up their cause.
1890 William Booth's *In Darkest England and the Way Out*.
Edwin Chadwick dies.
1891 Charles Booth's *Life and Labour of the People in London* (completed 1903).
1895 National Trust founded.
1901 Seebohm Rowntree's *Poverty: A Study of Town Life*.
Death of Queen Victoria. Edward VII comes to throne.

Useful Addresses

The Museum of Labour History, Limehouse Town Hall, Commercial Road, London, E.14.
The Salvation Army, Schools Information Service, International Headquarters, 101 Queen Victoria Street, London, EC4P 4EP.
Dr Barnardo's, Tenner's Lane, Barkingside, Ilford, Essex, IG6 1QG (they have a photographic archive).
The Shaftesbury Society, 112 Regent Street, Westminster, London SW1P 4AX.

Places to Visit

Saltaire. Very much the same as when Titus Salt conceived it. Take Reynolds *Guide to Saltaire* with you when you walk round.
York. The city is worth a visit in itself. Many of the streets that Rowntree surveyed still remain.
Birmingham. Parts of Chamberlain's redevelopment can be seen, but there has been a lot of modern development due to the motor car and modern shopping needs.
London. This Dickens House Museum, 48 Doughty Street, W.C.1. (open Monday – Saturday 10.00 a.m. – 5.00 p.m.).

Biographical Notes

DR BARNARDO (1845–1905). Born in Dublin. Originally intended to practise as a medical missionary in China, but the meeting with Jim Jarvis changed the direction of his life. During his lifetime he raised £3.25 million, established various homes and rescued 60,000 boys and girls. A notice outside each hostel read "No destitute child ever refused."

BESANT, Annie (1847–1933). Born in London. Became a socialist and supporter of social reform. Advocated the use of birth control, for which she was condemned by many Victorians. In 1889 she was converted to Hinduism and in 1916 founded the Indian Home Rule League which pressed for Indian independence.

BOOTH, Charles (1840–1916). Born in Liverpool to a prosperous family, and became rich in shipping. Became interested in social issues when he moved to London in 1880s. Concerned about poverty and unemployment and that London, a city of four million people, had no local government until 1888. His survey of London was published in 17 volumes.

BOOTH, William (1829–1919). Born in Nottingham into a poor family. Became a Methodist preacher but left in 1861 to become an evangelist. In 1865 he began mission work in London and in 1878 founded the Salvation Army to help the poor and also convert them to Christianity. His message was not always popular but the Army grew and is today represented in 83 countries.

CHADWICK, Edwin (1800–90). Born in Manchester. Trained as a lawyer in London and, when qualified, visited prisons, workhouses, and slums. Came under the influence of the utilitarians, believing in progress and reform, seeking efficiency and cheapness. Served the Poor Law authorities and Public Health for 20 years, working 10-12 hours every day.

CHAMBERLAIN, Joseph (1836–1914). Born in London, and joined the family's prosperous screw-making business. In 1869 he joined the National Education League and became its leading light, pressing for education that was universal, compulsory and free. Between 1873 and 1876 served as Birmingham's reforming mayor. In 1876 he entered the House of Commons as Liberal M.P., but later allied with the Conservatives and became Colonial Secretary.

DICKENS, Charles (1812–70). Born in Portsmouth, the son of a navy clerk. Spent his boyhood in Chatham, but his father was imprisoned for debt and he was sent to work in a blacking warehouse at the age of 12. This experience influenced his early writings. Later became an office boy, and court reporter for the *Morning Chronicle*. His first success as a novelist came with *The Pickwick Papers*, which was published in 20 monthly instalments in 1836. Continued writing until his death in 1870, leaving his last novel *The Mystery of Edwin Drood* unfinished.

GREENWOOD, James (1852–1929). Born in London, the son of a coach-builder. Became a journalist and novelist writing for the *Pall Mall Gazette* of which his brother was the first editor. Also wrote for the *Daily Telegraph*. He was sympathetic to the plight of the poor, and often wandered round the slums in disguise, so that he could write from first-hand observation and contact.

HILL, Octavia (1838–1912). Born in Wisbech, Cambridgeshire. Using borrowed money she established the first of her housing projects in London in 1864. In 1884 she was put in charge of the Church Commissioners' property in Southwark, where she trained other women to manage housing owned by the Church. Her interest in urban problems led her into the open space movement, which resulted in the foundation in 1895 of the National Trust, of which she was one of the founder members.

HILL, Rowland (1795–1879). Born in Kidderminster and ran his father's school until he was 30. Was active in the campaign for the reform of Parliament, and became Secretary of a society to encourage emigration to Australia. Also active in the Society for the Diffusion of Useful Knowledge, which aimed to bring cheap worthwhile books to a broad section of the population. Invented a printing machine. Best known for his Post Office Reform and the introduction of the Penny Post.

KAY-SHUTTLEWORTH, Sir James (1804–77). Born Rochdale, where his father was a cotton manufacturer. Trained as a doctor in Manchester, where his experiences and work made him aware of social problems. Became a Poor Law Commissioner in East Anglia and then Secretary to the Committee of Council on Education. Introduced school inspectors and the pupil-teacher system. This led him to establish a training college for teachers in Battersea.

KINGSLEY, Charles (1819–75). Born at Holne in Devon. Entered the Church, and became active in the movement for social reform and was one of the founders of Christian Socialism. Many of his novels are well known and include *The Water Babies* (1863), *Hereward the Wake* (1866) and *Westward Ho* (1855).

MAYHEW, Henry (1812–87). Born London, the son of a solicitor. Ran away to sea and made a voyage to India. On his return studied law with his father and later turned to journalism. One of the founders of the humorous magazine *Punch* in 1841 and for two years its joint editor. From the 1840s became increasingly interested in social problems and the poor. In 1849-50 became a journalist for the *Morning Chronicle*. Left paper to begin work on *London Labour and the London Poor* (1851). His methods of using interviews and questionnaires were taken up and developed by later sociologists.

NIGHTINGALE, Florence (1820–1910). Trained as nurse in Germany in 1850 and sent to Scutari in 1854. Death rate brought down in the hospital from 42 per 100 to 2.2. In 1855 the Nightingale Fund for training nurses was established and in 1856 the Medical Staff Corps was formed. Once in England again she pressed hard for a Royal Commission on the health of the army, and this was set up in 1857. In 1860 she established the Nightingale School for Nurses at St Thomas's Hospital in London. Belatedly she was honoured with the Order of Merit in 1907, the first woman to receive the award.

ROWNTREE, Seebohm (1871–1954). Born High Wycombe, Bucks. Became Chairman of the family chocolate company. Was interested in social problems and also industrial relations. His survey of York became a classic of its kind. Conducted three surveys of York. Was able to add to the work of Booth because he used professionals such as dieticians and physiologists to determine what weight, height and diet should be. His work and ideas were a great influence upon the reforming Liberal government which came to power in 1906, and in particular upon David Lloyd George.

SALT, Titus (1803–76). Born in Morley, Yorkshire where his father was in the wool trade. First to use donskoi and alpaca wool. His model town contained many progressive and caring features. The park by the Aire was 14 acres in size, the club and institute provided a large library, evening classes and lectures, in addition to chess and billiards. However, no beer-shops or public houses were allowed.

SHAFTESBURY, Anthony Ashley Cooper, 7th Earl of (1811–85). Probably the leading social reformer of the Victorian period. His interests and achievements were varied and included the Lunacy Act of 1845, which did much to prevent the insane being regarded as social outcasts. Was very active in the Factory Reform Movement, seeking to improve conditions and to reduce hours of work. Urban conditions and housing, the education of the poor all concerned him. An active Christian throughout his life and believed it the duty of the better off to help the poor.

WEBB, Beatrice (1858–1943). Born Beatrice Potter into a wealthy Gloucestershire family. Father Chairman of the Great Western Railway. Went into journalism and worked for Charles Booth, and later for Octavia Hill in the Charity Organisation Society. Was increasingly drawn into working conditions of the labouring population, which she publicized through her writings. Married Sidney Webb in 1892. Both active Fabian socialists in 1890s and later played a prominent part in the Labour Party. Together they founded the London School of Economics (part of the University of London) and also the *New Statesman*. In 1909 she was a member of the Royal Commission on the Poor Law.

Money

New Money	Old Money
1p.	2.4d.
2½p.	6d. (sixpence)
5p.	1s. 0d. (1 shilling)
12½p.	2s. 6d. (half a crown)
50p.	10s. 0d. (ten shillings)

Always look at what money and wages could buy rather than at what seem low prices to us. It is no use butter being 4p a pound if we only earn 50p a week. Remember that there were 12 old pence (d.) in a shilling (s.) and 20 shillings to the pound.